WEATHER STATION

by Daphne Greaves
illustrated by Necdet Yilmaz

SCHOOL PUBLISHERS

Printed in China

ISBN 10: 0-15-350787-X
ISBN 13: 978-0-15-350787-8

Ordering Options
ISBN 10: 0-15-350601-6 (Grade 4 On-Level Collection)
ISBN 13: 978-0-15-350601-7 (Grade 4 On-Level Collection)
ISBN 10: 0-15-357924-2 (package of 5)
ISBN 13: 978-0-15-357924-0 (package of 5)

2 3 4 5 6 7 8 9 10 985 12 11 10 09 08 07

Characters

Ms. Lee	**Jamal**	**Mr. Kelly**
Mia	**George**	**Pablo**
Stacy	**Chrissy**	

Setting: A weather station

Ms. Lee: Mr. Kelly, thank you for letting us inspect the weather station.

Mr. Kelly: We meteorologists love company.

Ms. Lee: Class, who can define the word *meteorologist*?

Pablo: That's someone who studies the weather.

Mr. Kelly: Nice going, Pablo. Now who would like to read a sentence off the blackboard and tell us what it means? Jamal?

Jamal: *It's raining cats and dogs.* That means it's raining very hard.

Ms. Lee: Good job. George, read the next one, please.

George: *It's spitting snow.*

Ms. Lee: What does that mean?

George: I don't know, but it sounds messy!

Ms. Lee: Mr. Kelly, George tends to be a bit exuberant. He's our class clown.

George: I am funny.

Ms. Lee: Yes, you are. However, I'd like you to nurture your more serious side in class.

Mr. Kelly: Let's make a deal, George. Work now and play later. At the end of our visit, you can tell a joke.

George: It's a deal!

George: I guess *spitting snow* means it's only snowing a little bit. I guess it means snow flurries.

Mr. Kelly: I am impressed, George.

Ms. Lee: What do the sentences have in common?

Mia: They describe a type of weather.

Ms. Lee: That's right. How often do we talk about the weather?

Pablo: All the time. People will say it's a beautiful day.

Chrissy: We tell each other when it's going to rain or snow.

Ms. Lee: Why do we talk about the weather so much?

Chrissy: It's important. If it's going to be cold, I'll wear a sweater.

Jamal: If it's going to be hot, I'll wear shorts.

Ms. Lee: The weather inspires us to wear certain clothes. It's also an important part of making other decisions. Farmers study the weather when they plant crops.

Mr. Kelly: Sailors keep an eye on the weather all the time. They want to make sure they don't get caught in a storm out at sea.

Ms. Lee: Can anyone think of a weather story that made news?

Mia: Hurricane Katrina. That was a big weather story.

Ms. Lee: Who can give us a general definition of weather?

George: It's what you find when you stick your head out the window.

Mr. Kelly: Well, George does make a good point. Weather is simply the condition of the atmosphere at a particular place and time.

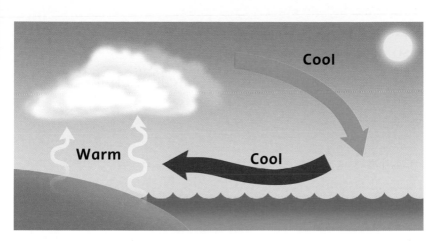

Stacy: You mean like whether it's hot or cold?

Mr. Kelly: That's right. What other kinds of weather conditions are there?

Jamal: Wet and dry.

Pablo: Windy or calm.

Mr. Kelly: All these conditions make up our weather.

Ms. Lee: Could you explain some more?

Mr. Kelly: As the sun heats the Earth, the air is warmed.

Ms. Lee: Class, remember what happens to air as it warms?

Pablo: It rises.

Mr. Kelly: Exactly, and cool air sinks. The cool air rushes in to fill the space underneath the warm air.

Stacy: Is that what causes the wind?

Mr. Kelly: That's right. Now heat from the sun also causes water to evaporate.

Ms. Lee: What happens to water when it evaporates?

Pablo: It turns into a vapor.

Mr. Kelly: Yes, and this vapor then becomes part of the air. It forms clouds. Now as warm air continues to rise, it cools. The vapor in the clouds then turns back into water and—

George: It rains!

Ms. Lee: Or snows, sleets, or hails.

Mia: The weather changes because air gets warm and then cools.

Jamal: Don't forget about water evaporating and turning into clouds.

Stacy: Then it turns back into water again.

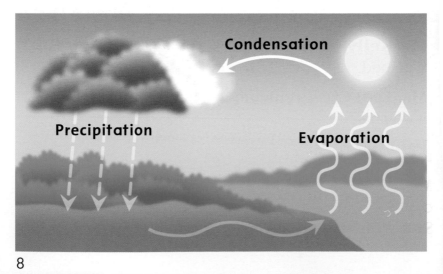

George: Why is it that sometimes we get a terrible hurricane?

Mr. Kelly: Hurricanes begin over the ocean during the summer when the water is warm. The air over the water gets warm and rises. In a hurricane, the warm air rises rapidly. It creates strong winds. The wind and heavy rain of a hurricane are much stronger than an ordinary rainstorm.

Ms. Lee: Weather forecasters have to be very flexible since the weather can change at any time. They must cease whatever they were doing when this happens and get to work!

Mr. Kelly: Telling people about dangerous weather is my most important job. When vulnerable people know what's coming they can move to safety.

Chrissy: How do meteorologists know what tomorrow's weather will be?

Mr. Kelly: Meteorologists comprehend that certain conditions lead to certain kinds of weather. Sometimes we're wrong, but often we get it right.

Cumulus cloud

Pablo: I've heard that one way to predict weather is to scan the sky for clouds.

Mr. Kelly: That's true. I want to show you a few things, so everybody lumber on over here and encircle the table. Can you squeeze into that small space, George?

George: Sure, I'm very pliable and nimble.

Mr. Kelly: Excellent vocabulary, George! Now, as I was saying, different kinds of clouds bring different weather. Look at this picture of a cloud.

George: It's big and puffy, and it almost looks delicate, like it would make a nice pillow.

Mr. Kelly: This is called a *cumulus* cloud. When you see a solitary cloud or two, that means you can expect nice weather.

Mia: What if you see a lot of clouds?

Mr. Kelly: If you see a lot of big clouds bunched together, you better get out your umbrella.

Ms. Lee: Look at this picture of a cloud. Will you describe it for us, Stacy?

Stacy: Well, it's not part of a bunch of clouds. It's more like a blanket that covers the whole sky. It looks like it needs to be untangled.

Mr. Kelly: It's called a *stratus* cloud. That was a very good description.

Mr. Kelly: Stratus clouds just bring a little rain or drizzle. Many times stratus clouds appear in the morning and then clear up.

Jamal: Wow, so by looking at the clouds you can tell what the weather will be?

Stratus clouds

Ms. Lee: Meteorologists also have some helpful tools. Some of them are right here on this table. This looks familiar. I'll bet some of you have seen this before.

Mia: My grandparents have one on their barn. It's a weather vane!

Mr. Kelly: That's right. Weather vanes turn in the wind. They tell us the direction from which the wind is coming. This can give us clues about coming weather. For example, winds from the south are often warm. They are also wetter than winds from the north.

Ms. Lee: I'm sure everyone knows what this is.

The Class: A thermometer!

Mr. Kelly: Right again. Thermometers have a tube containing a red liquid. The liquid is either colored alcohol or mercury. As the liquid warms it expands. As it cools, the liquid shrinks. The level of the liquid shows the current temperature.

Ms. Lee: What temperature is freezing?

Mia: Thirty-two degrees Fahrenheit or zero degrees Celsius.

Chrissy: Brrrrr! That's cold.

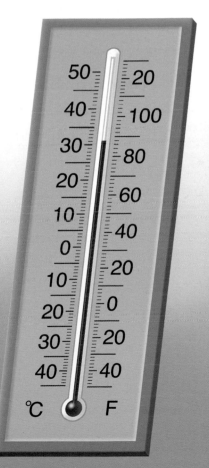

Mr. Kelly: Ms. Lee, you have a great and unique class, and I think they learned a lot.

Ms. Lee: I agree. George, I'm very proud of your mature behavior.

George: Thanks, Ms. Lee.

Mr. Kelly: So, George, I'm sure you are not reluctant to tell your joke now.

George: What happens when it rains cats and dogs?

The Class: What?

George: You have to be careful not to step in a poodle.

The Class: Oh, no! That's terrible!

Think Critically

1. Why does the class visit Mr. Kelly?

2. How does a weather vane give clues about coming weather?

3. How does Mr. Kelly keep George from being funny while he is talking?

4. What does the author probably think about the work of meteorologists?

5. What did you learn about the weather from this book?

Science

Weather Report What was it like outside today? Write a paragraph describing today's weather. Be sure to use as many weather terms as you can.

 School-Home Connection Read this Readers' Theater with a family member. Look at the pictures of cumulus and stratus clouds. Then watch for clouds in the sky and try to identify them.

Word Count: 1,243 (1,253)